HMS *DIDO*

When Germany surrendered its navy in May 1945, it did so aboard HMS *Dido* — a fitting reward for the gallant cruiser. She had seen action in many of the major naval engagements in the Mediterranean and North Atlantic (a war-service record that is second to none). However, she rarely receives a mention in any World War II publications. Eric Jeffs proudly served aboard HMS *Dido* (September 1940 - January 1946), and his fond recollections do great justice to one of the Royal Navy's 'forgotten' heroines.

Dedication

This book is dedicated to the memory of all those who served in the ship during WW2, especially to those who did not return, having died at Crete or on other operations.

Secondly, to the good people of Bolton who rose so magnificently to the challenge of 'Warship's Week' in 1941.

Acknowledgements

To Councillor John Walsh, Bolton's mayor in 2002, who first suggested I record my memoirs for posterity.

To my dear wife, Catherine, who valiantly struggled through my handwritten notes to make sense of them and transfer them to her computer.

To our two daughter, Hilary and Claire and their families, who have helped and encouraged me through the three years it has taken to complete the task.

Last, but not least — to my publishers, Arthur H. Stockwell Ltd., who have produced a first-class presentation of my story and made the whole project worthwhile.

My heartfelt thanks to everyone concerned.

Eric Jeffs

HMS *DIDO*

A Tiffy's Tale

Eric Jeffs ERA MID

(HMS *Dido* —10/9/40-10/1/46)

ARTHUR H. STOCKWELL LTD.
Torrs Park   Ilfracombe   Devon
Established 1898
www.ahstockwell.co.uk

British Library Cataloguing-in-Publication Data.
A catalogue record for this book is available
from the British Library.

ISBN 0 7223 3706-X
Printed in Great Britain by
Arthur H. Stockwell Ltd.
Torrs Park   Ilfracombe
Devon

HMS Dido

The Ship's Crest

Described in heraldic terms as 'issuant from the flames proper on a blue field'. It is derived from Virgil's story and the mythology of Dido, founder and Queen of Carthage. Legend tells us that, after her lover Aeneas left Carthage at the command of the gods, she threw herself on a funeral pyre in despair at being forsaken.

Contents

PART 1

Our War at Sea

In World War II the government instituted a 'Warship Week' when the British people were invited to subscribe to the cost of a warship. The townspeople of Bolton magnificently raised in excess of £1,000,000 in less than a week. Their reward was HMS *Dido*. This led to a great comradeship between the town and the ship, eventually leading to the ship's company being granted the Freedom of the Borough of Bolton on April 14th 1973. They even named the Sea Cadet headquarters *Dido*. As events were to prove, they had every reason to be proud of their ship. In May 2002 I visited the Mayor of Bolton and was privileged to be given a guided tour of the splendid display of *Dido* memorabilia in the town hall.

At the request of Councillor Walsh, Bolton's mayor (2002-2003), who entertained my wife and me to morning tea and conducted us around the '*Dido* Suite', I am happy to record some memories of my five years' service in the ship:

Memories and Random Thoughts! Apart from a few old newspaper cuttings, some faint and well-worn internal notices and some photographs, I have no other literature (official or otherwise) or diaries to which I can refer. I have to rely on my memories — some happy, some not. Names of ships and personnel I remember so well, though in many cases I prefer them to remain anonymous. It was a long time ago, so naturally some details are a little hazy, but nevertheless unforgettable.

Before joining HMS *Dido*, I served aboard the repair ship *Sandhurst* in Dover harbour, during the 'Dunkirk period'. I had just returned from mid-week leave when, after completing some small repairs, I decided to return them to the destroyer *Codrington*, which was alongside. Not seeing anyone aboard I returned to *Sandhurst*. Within minutes there was an air raid in which *Codrington* was sunk and *Sandhurst* flooded and later abandoned. After a week's 'survivor's' leave, it was back to Chatham Barracks, but not for long as I was soon to be drafted to *Dido*. Would my luck last? I was very apprehensive.

At 5.00 a.m. on September 10th 1940, some 400 officers and ratings left Chatham Royal Naval Barracks en route to Cammel Laird's shipyard, Birkenhead, to commission HMS *Dido*. Meanwhile, having joined the Royal Navy the previous February at the invitation of HM Government for the duration of the war (Hostilities Only), I too was drafted to *Dido* as an engine room artificer (ERA or 'Tiffy') at Cammel Laird's. Most of my new messmates were from the 400 who were Royal Navy-trained or time-serving personnel. We HOs were not very welcome, but as our numbers increased we eventually became friendly and united — as much as human nature would allow in the confines of a small ship. I still correspond with a particular pal (a 'regular') I met again over forty years later at the Bolton Reunion of 1991.

When first commissioned, HMS *Dido* was a light ack-ack cruiser of 5,500 tons with a main armament of 5.25" guns in four twin turrets, with a secondary armament of one 4" star-shell gun, pom-poms, smaller close-range weapons and six torpedo tubes. The main (64,000 HP) engines had a top speed of 30 knots. The ship carried a wartime complement of 550 ship's company.

We first sailed under the command of Captain H. W. U. McCall, who was previously naval attaché in South America. He played a great part in the scuttling of the German pocket battleship *Graf Spee*. In his first address to the ship's company, most of whom, including myself, had never been to sea before, he said that he insisted on a clean ship and a happy ship with strong discipline, which would combine to make an efficient ship. This he achieved, though of course there were inevitably some dissidents from time to time who were summarily dealt with. As usual in warships, there is rivalry between the gunnery and engine-room departments as to the true main armament, the 5.25" guns or the 4 HP turbines. Time will tell.

Unfortunately, my first overnight leave was disastrous, to say the least. As my home was on Merseyside, I took the opportunity to spend the night there. The ship was under sailing orders and was being moved to Bidston Dock, further down the river. Sadly, I overslept, so that at the time I should have been on board I was just boarding a train at my local station. I went first to Cammel Laird's only to find *Dido* had already left, so I had to make my own way to Bidston Dock, arriving before the ship. However, my reasons for being absent without leave were not acceptable and I suffered the penalty of a few days' leave stoppage.

While we were there Liverpool experienced a heavy air raid. It was eerie and unnerving to watch an oil-cake warehouse and a sugar warehouse ablaze on the other side of the river. Our guns were used, but without success. This was the only time I was to see a city blitzed — an unforgettable experience. I did manage to snatch some home leave before we left for Scapa Flow and our uncertain future.

CHAPTER 1

FIRST COMMISSION
September 1940 - October 1942

After a period of trials, tribulations and exercises, the ship joined the Home fleet at Scapa Flow. It was a sombre sight to see the wrecks of ships of the German Imperial Navy of World War I still visible above these waters, close to the wreck of HMS *Royal Oak.* Our first major task was to escort the aircraft carrier *Furious,* which was ferrying aircraft to Freetown in Sierra Leone and Takoradi on the Gold Coast. We also had an escort of two destroyers. The aircraft were being sent to the Eastern Desert for use by General Wavell in his attack on the enemy. On the way south we had something of a scare when word was received that the German pocket battleship *Admiral von Scheer* was at sea in the Atlantic. *Furious* signalled that she had six aircraft to spare — Blackburn Rocs, Fairey Fulmars and Blackburn Skuas. With our mighty peashooters and what the two old destroyers had, we would have stood no chance. Shortly after the receipt of the signal, smoke was seen on the horizon. You can well imagine our thoughts and fears, but it was a Spanish fishing vessel. So we went on our merry way without further incident.

However, we were having problems in the engine-room department. We junior ERAs had never seen a boiler room before, and knew little about them, least of all how to change a burst gauge glass; but we soon learned — the hard way — with the help of stoker petty officers. Time after time, watch by watch, the gauges were bursting with monotonous regularity. By the time we arrived back at Scapa Flow we had exhausted our supply of gauge glasses. Though some of the more senior (regular) ERAs thought so, it was not our (HO's) fault. Shortly afterwards we had just started boiler cleaning, when we received the order to replace all equipment and prepare for sea. We sailed in the early hours of the morning to Wallsend slipway for a short refit to correct some engine defects, during which it was found that the gauge-glass mountings had been incorrectly fitted, which proved our seniors wrong. After the refit burst gauge glasses were rare. We were able to snatch a few days' leave, during which I and many others received telegrams extending our leave by four days. We were not to know that it was to be our last for two and a half years, and unhappily for some crew members, their last ever. Whilst in the dockyard we had a visit from HRH the Duke of Kent, who came into our mess very briefly when there were only a few of us present. He was later killed when serving in the RAF.

The first few months of 1941 were taken up by Atlantic convoys. These turned out to be not uneventful, but we did not lose a single ship in any of ours. Of course, strong gales and rough seas caused many problems — merchant ships losing their place and causing us to backtrack in order to escort them back into position. One such convoy caused much concern. The commander, who was well liked by the ship's company, noticed that one of the seaboats was not properly secured. As he went to inspect it the ship lurched and he was thrown against the davits, suffering very serious injuries, necessitating a stay in hospital — happily returning to the ship later. If heavy seas in the Atlantic were a problem, fog was even worse, particularly in narrow waters, as when escorting a convoy through the Bristol Channel. Fog, though, does help to diminish the danger from enemy submarines and aircraft; but with little room to manoeuvre and no radar for merchant vessels (just sirens and men stationed on the bows) there was always the danger of collisions.

Having negotiated the Bristol Channel at the breathtaking speed of 3 knots, we proceeded through the Irish Sea, heading for Liverpool (the merchant ships, that is); but to our disgust, dismay and disappointment, *Dido* was destined for other duties.

We left Scapa Flow in April, first to Glasgow, passing HMS *Hood* with never a thought that we would not see her again, nor our homes, for two and a half years. Officially, we knew not where we were bound for, except that lashed on deck were crates marked 'RN Dockyard, Gibraltar' and 'RN Stores, Malta'. Leaving the stores at Gibraltar and Malta, we finally arrived in Alexandria to join the Mediterranean fleet. Following further exercises with our new fleet, we became exceedingly efficient in all departments.

May 1941 was a mixture of triumph and tragedy. The situation in Greece and Crete had deteriorated. 15th Cruiser Squadron (*Orion*, *Dido* and *Ajax*) was assigned the task of covering North and Eastern Crete. On May 21st/22nd we met and destroyed a seaborne invasion of Crete, consisting of a number of small ships, a destroyer and some 2,500 men. The following morning, when clear of the action, it was noticed that *Orion* had an unusual bow wave:

[Message from *Dido* to *Orion* — 'Have you received some damage for'ard?'
Reply from *Orion* to *Dido* — 'No! Just a couple of bodies caught in our PV chains, they'll clear away eventually.']

At the westerly end of Crete it was a different story. Many ships were damaged or sunk in air attacks, among them the cruisers *Fiji* and *Gloucester*, not forgetting Lord Mountbatten's *Kelly*.

Meanwhile, with gun barrels red-hot from continuous firing at German Stukas and Italian bombers, we were at Heraklion to load a consignment of Greek gold. It was taken aboard with the Stukas screaming over. The boxes of gold were stored in Q magazine, but just as the magazine hatch was being opened, another air raid started. One box was hurriedly dropped, and burst open. The ship's company had to leave it to leap to action stations

In company with some destroyers and a small merchant ship, carrying 400 wounded, we left to return to Alexandria, hoping to complete the storage of the boxes. Some hope! In the Kaso Straits, one ship was having trouble with her engines and lagged behind. We signalled her and got no reply. Then she stopped dead. We asked the skipper, through the loudhailer, what was the matter, A dour Scots voice came bellowing back though a megaphone, "We've broken down — I cannot get any reply from my engine room."

Our commanding officer, Captain H. W. U. McCall, replied with a hurried signal: 'Have all your wounded ready for disembarking immediately. If you are not away in ten minutes, we propose to torpedo you.'

Within an incredibly short time, smoke was belching from the steamer's funnels and she was sprinting ahead at about 16 knots — well above her normal speed. She still sent us no signal. Then the first wave of Stukas came over — one stick of bombs fell right round the merchant ship and she disappeared from view, to reappear moments later steaming placidly. We spelled out one word — '**P-H-E-W**'. We continued to be attacked all that day, and again the guns were red-hot. It was only when we arrived back in Alexandria that we remembered that the stowage of the gold had not been completed. This was promptly carried out, and when the contents of the burst box were swept up with a broom, not one coin was missing.

While in Suda Bay we saw the superstructure of HMS *York*, sunk a few days earlier by German bombs. *York* revived some memories for me. She was the first warship I had ever seen — alongside Liverpool landing stage — was I ever to see another one? Earlier in the year 1939, the government introduced conscription for the first time during peacetime. I was among the first to register as a militiaman, as we were then known, and stated a preference for the Royal Navy.

My thoughts were suddenly interrupted by an air-raid warning. A group of about five of us were on deck looking towards the wreck, and we dashed for the bulkhead door leading to our mess, all trying at the same time to get through a space normally allowing one at a time. We ended up on the deck, but apart from injured pride no harm was done. It was a false alarm!

On May 28th we sailed again for Crete to cover the evacuation of our troops. The C.-in-C.'s message to us was 'We must not let the army down — you will have air support.' The plan was for destroyers to embark troops in the harbour, transfer them to the cruisers and be clear of the Kaso Straits by dawn. This was the base for Stuka dive-bombers. Unfortunately the plan went wrong. *Ajax* had been hit the previous evening and returned to Alexandria. Two destroyers, *Hereward* and *Imperial*, were damaged and had to be sunk.

We were thus delayed by two hours, and instead of being clear of the straits by dawn we were right in the middle. Although we managed to destroy some aircraft, the AA control officer remarked, "I see no future in this."

At approximately 08.15 (our gunners shot down some Stukas — they couldn't miss, there were so many) we received a direct hit which destroyed B turret, killing some fifty men (soldiers and sailors). In reality, we were seconds from total disaster — had the bomb hit the bridge it would have penetrated further and blown the ship apart — and this story could not have been written. Fortunately the engines were not damaged — we escaped at high speed and were soon beyond Stuka range.

Our promised air support arrived many hours late from Alexandria, some thirty miles away. But for the superb skill and seamanship of Captain McCall we would not have survived. And yet he apologised to the ship's company, saying that although he managed to dodge eight Stukas, he did not see a ninth, coming at us from astern. It was to be the last bomb that plane dropped, as he finished ahead of us in the sea. I have been specially asked to record my own personal memories of this action, so reluctantly here they are:

I came off watch in the boiler room at 08.00 and took up my position as Flooding ERA at Q magazine, which meant that if it were damaged I would be ordered to flood or 'spray' the magazine. But it was B magazine I had to flood, passing by the turret as I did so. I had sensed that the ERA in that position was a casualty, but it was some time before I realised I had been standing by the bulkhead door, and how narrowly I had escaped the same fate. By now the area was on fire and the marines' mess deck, strewn with bodies, was awash from the hoses of the fire party who had the fire well under control. A few minutes later I had to 'spray' Q magazine, having first removed a dead stoker from off the valves — a commonplace task, happening many times in many ships. The surgeon commander and sickbay staff must be commended for the way they carried out their gruesome task of coping with the casualties. So too must the two chief stokers (fortified by the navy's favourite tonic) who spent most of the day stitching dead bodies into sacks for burial at sea — some untouched, like the stoker, some mangled almost beyond recognition. The ERA in the fire party was subsequently awarded the DSM. To this day I can 'see' the wounded and frightened men, and 'hear' their cries — some adrift in water from the fire hoses. In fact I almost stepped on one disembowelled body. It was not my happiest hour on the ship. In fact, had the bomb struck a few seconds earlier, I would have been directly underneath it, and this tale would not have been told. This happened often to ships in similar circumstances. My assignment had been part of regular damage control, which is part of the administration of a ship. It must be efficient. So, as we had carried out countless exercises to ensure efficiency, we knew exactly what to do when the occasion arose. Quite simply — no efficient damage control, no ship? This was to be proved correct later in another cruiser. However, *Dido*'s forward fire party was quick to respond, soon dealt with the fire in the turret and flooded the marines' mess deck and canteen flat where I was stationed. The commander was quick to arrive at the mess deck to ask me what action had been taken. When I explained, he remarked, "Well done! Who are you?" That was the only conversation I had about the incident until two and a half years later — not even with the engineer's office, or anyone else when I come to think about it. I certainly didn't talk about it — my family did not know for a number of years. It was a routine job that had to be done. Captain McCall was still in control of the ship — that was enough for us

On our return to Alexandria the C.-in-C. came aboard to inspect the ship. He was heard to say, "Mere superficial damage — I will have you at sea again in a week." As we were completely exhausted, his words were not well received.

Within a day or so we were at sea again, heading eastward to Port Said and the Suez Canal for the first time — quite an experience. Sailing further south, we arrived at Perim Island at the south of the Red Sea. The object of this exercise was to bombard the port of Assab in Italian-held Eritrea, and land troops from an Indian frigate. Eventually our marines went ashore and the Italians surrendered. The next port of call was Mombassa, to leave some of our scrap metal behind; then on to Durban, where we had more effective repairs carried out. En route we heard that the Germans had attacked Russia. After three weeks in Durban there was a weekend in Cape Town and Simonstown — still not knowing our final destination. Heading northward into the Atlantic, we spent a few hours at St Helena, then a weekend in Port of Spain, Trinidad, being challenged by USS *Omaha* on the way. At last we discovered our final stop — Brooklyn Navy Yard, New York — arriving there on August 9th, when we unloaded the Greek gold. This was to be a memorable phase in our lives. The Americans were very friendly and extremely kind to us. Captain McCall held a press conference on board and spoke of our exploits to date. During this time the ship had an extensive refit. B turret was renewed and a Q turret fitted — this being as originally designed — and our radar was updated. Electrical equipment, boiler rooms, etc. had defects repaired. After a few days' exercises off Rhode Island we returned to the navy yard for extra engine repairs and various electrical adjustments. Of course we still had to carry out our own work and duties — part of the overnight duty of the engine room being to check security and any fire hazard. As we visited the boiler room it was quite usual to hear a voice behind the boiler — "I'll see ya baby," from a group of men playing poker — or the unmistakeable sound of a noisy sleeper. That was their problem, not ours. However, the repairs were completed on time. Some ship's company was changed as well.

Next was a week in Bermuda for training and exercise. Just after we left Bermuda the Japanese bombed Pearl Harbor, bringing the USA into the war, so they were now officially allies. We did have an alarm while heading eastward. An American warship failed to recognise us. Were we heading back to UK, as we hoped? Not likely — it was straight back to Gibraltar, where, owing to a navigational error, we had to steam around for twelve anxious hours before entering harbour, then on to Malta, where we spent a miserable Christmas; and back to Alexandria for New Year's Day.

On our return to the Med we heard of the sinking of HMS *Barham*, torpedoed off Alexandria. "Impossible!" said the C.-in-C. "There are no submarines here." But there were many, as subsequent events and sinkings proved. "Bye-bye, *Barham*!" Captain McCall, being a Scot, requested to 'go out of routine' for the New Year — an excuse for some members of the ship's company to make up for Christmas.

1942 — The year started very quietly. We were exercising with the ships *Naiad* and *Euryalus*, both *Dido*-class cruisers. One evening we were sent to sea as it was rumoured that an Italian cruiser was at sea. It turned out to be *Cleopatra*, so we had four *Dido*-class cruisers together — WONDERFUL! — but not for long, as shortly afterwards *Naiad* was torpedoed and sunk just ahead of us — another narrow escape. This was to be one of many over the next two and a half years or so.

In February we bombarded the island of Rhodes, thus adding more rubble to the legendary ancient ruins.

For a while we bombarded the North African coast at El Daba

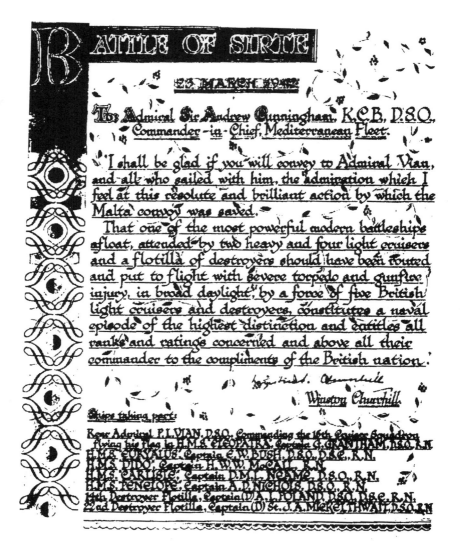

Citation from Winston Churchill on the Battle of Sirte

and Mersa Matruh in support of the army, with some success. We then began a series of Alexandria-to-Malta convoys, dubbing them 'Club Runs' as they became so regular. We would leave on Friday night, escorting full merchant ships about halfway, handing them over to another escort to Malta and returning to Alexandria with empty ones. These trips were gruelling and hazardous. Of course the Germans soon realised what was happening — partially through some of their friends in Alexandria. They would attack us about 10.30 a.m. on Saturday and 9.30 a.m. on Sunday. None of this was widely reported in the press until the occasion when we left Alexandria on March 20th at the usual time. It was to be somewhat different and more difficult. The Italian Navy, in their wisdom, decided to join in, ultimately suffering a humiliating defeat. This was to become known as the Second Battle of Sirte, and for once it was well reported. At this stage I must point out that we in the engine-room department knew little of what was happening 'upstairs'. We could only guess, and at times it was quite frightening. All we could hear was gunfire, shells and bombs all around us. Although *Dido* was not damaged, other ships were. *Cleopatra* was put out of action, and, when he learned that he was now senior officer, Captain McCall took over command of the operation. After some of their ships, including a Vittorio-class cruiser and a destroyer were sunk or badly damaged, the Italian fleet withdrew and never put to sea again. Captain McCall was later awarded the DSO for his gallantry and leadership, and the ship received a citation from Prime Minister Churchill.

As a postscript to the Battle of Sirte, a new messmate who joined the ship told me the following story. He was in the destroyer *Zulu* when she was sunk off Tobruk. He was captured and interrogated by Italian officers who told him it was unnecessary to name his ship, as they already knew. "Oh, yes, *Zulu*! We knew you were in the second Battle of Sirte. We would have won that battle, but the sea was so rough and our sailors so seasick they had to withdraw." The sea could be a little unkind at times. One wave did, in fact, move a torpedo off its cradle just as it was about to be launched — the 'tin fish' that didn't get away. Captain McCall was not amused, but the engine room were, much to the annoyance of the torpedo officer.

The convoys continued for a while until June, when it was considered unwise to continue. Many RN and merchant ships had been lost during that period, including the submarine depot ship, HMS *Medway*, which was not disclosed at the time. Why was she sailing alone? *Dido* was sent on a rescue mission and retrieved some torpedoes. Owing to the presence of U-boats in the area, we could not stay too long. The torpedo officer was in his element playing with his new toy, but we were somewhat apprehensive. We returned to Alexandria for a short while, by which time the German Army were within about thirty miles of the port. So this base was evacuated and we operated from Port Said and Haifa. This period did not see much activity, apart from some bombardments of the North African coast and a spell as AA guard in the Red Sea. Opportunities were granted, when in Haifa, to visit the Holy Land, and Cairo when in Suez.

We were soon to have an unpleasant surprise. It was time for Captain McCall to leave the ship at the end of his two-year appointment. It was a sad day for us all, though he was destined to gain higher rank, which he richly deserved. He was succeeded by Captain John Terry MVO.

CHAPTER 2

SECOND COMMISSION
October 1942 - October 1944

1942 — We knew nothing about Captain Terry. Another Captain McCall would have been too much to expect, but, as time would tell, Captain Terry gained the respect of the ship's company. Until now my story has been largely from memory, but I have some printed statistics for the next two years to which I can refer. Late October saw us in floating dock at Massawa in the Red Sea (where the temperature was 135°F in the shade) for minor repairs and a few days' leave in the cool hills of Asmara, Eritrea. Just after this, when we rejoined the fleet, a cruiser signalled to us, 'During our short time in the Med we have had thirty air attacks. Would you like some advice?'

Our reply was, 'During our time we have had 268 such attacks, nevertheless advice is welcome.'

We were still based at Suez — but not for long, for the 8th Army began their assault in North Africa towards El Alamein. Meanwhile HMSs *Coventry*, *Sikh* and *Zulu* had left Suez to shell Tobruk, but had all been sunk, as the enemy were waiting for them, having somehow obtained advance intelligence — no doubt from Port Said. On October 23rd General Montgomery started at El Alamein and swept rapidly westwards, freeing airfields for fighter cover, removing the menace of 'Bomb Alley' (except at Tobruk for a while) and opening up the eastern route to beleaguered Malta. At this time the ship was exercising with the fleet when we received the signal 'Detach from fleet. Assume independent command.' This meant we were on our own for a while, which was good, because carrying out fleet duties can sometimes be dull and monotonous. But where were we going? As we left the fleet the captain read out our instructions — we were to bombard Tobruk in order to destroy some enemy positions and port installations. The army couldn't get there as it was too difficult and the air force *would not*, saying it was too difficult for them also. To *Dido* — NO PROBLEM. Bombardments of this nature need to be very carefully planned and the whole ship's company in complete accord. For the gunnery to be effective, the engine's movements have to be exact, whether the ship is stopped or sailing at speed. In this we succeeded, accomplishing our objectives as required, with the result that the enemy surrendered Tobruk and the 8th Army entered the port, enabling them to prepare it for use once again as a supply base for our forces. This was the prelude to El Alamein. I have yet to see or hear any record or report of the navy's part in this episode of the war. 'Permission to rejoin fleet' was signalled. Even they didn't know when we had left and returned or where we had been.

Until November 15th the squadron had concentrated at Alexandria. On the 6th the North African landings had started in the Western Mediterranean, and the battle for control of the sea took on a new and far more hopeful aspect. On the 17th the squadron sailed from Alexandria with a convoy and delivered it intact to Malta, after which we returned to Alexandria, arriving on the 21st. On the 18th we had one air attack after dark and *Arethusa*, next astern of *Dido*, was hit by a torpedo, but managed to reach Alexandria under her own steam. On the 25th we sailed with yet another convoy to Malta, where we entered the Grand Harbour on the 27th. Neither the Italian fleet nor the German Air Force had attacked us. Malta was no longer a beleaguered fortress, and from then onwards convoys continued to arrive unmolested from the east.

On December 7th one cruiser was required to reinforce the 12th Cruiser Squadron in the Western Mediterranean. *Dido* was detailed and we left that night at top speed for Bone. Fortunately there was no moon and no one bothered us, though we passed the coast of Sicily, only nine miles away. Berthed in Bone harbour were *Sirius*, *Ashanti* and *Tartar*, forming a striking force to operate against enemy convoys and protect our own coastal traffic. On the 10th the force sailed for a sweep in the Sicilian Channel, having been steadily flared for half an hour, and so presumably reported to the enemy. We turned south-west at midnight, making for Algiers. About an hour later we realised that our shadowers had been friendly — RAF from Malta. On nearing the North African coast at dusk, the force was attacked by six bombers and four torpedo bombers, fortunately without damage. We secured alongside in Algiers during the forenoon of the 11th. On the 14th, *Argonaut* was torpedoed, but reached Algiers safely — we had been ordered to escort her, but were not needed.

During the period of the North African invasion, it was a well-known fact that many ships, from an aircraft carrier to destroyers were sunk or very badly damaged by torpedoes or mines, but *Dido* survived — just. I happened to be near the end of my spell on watch in the engine room when we received the order 'Full Ahead', which was most unusual.

The ship lurched and shuddered, and when my relief arrived he asked, "I suppose you were wondering what that was all about? Two torpedoes passed either side of us and exploded ashore."

That didn't make me feel any better. The force left for Bone on the 15th, our duties being divided between AA guard and exercises at Bone and Algiers. During this period there were a few light raids on the harbour at Bone, the weather being too bad for anything more. On the 19th the starboard outer propeller was damaged when coming into contact with an uncharted part of the jetty. We sailed from Bone on the 23rd, escorting *Circassia* to Algiers, by which time our potato supplies were getting low (we even tried to beg some from *Circassia*, without success) so we had to make do with various forms of rice balls — boiled, fried, whatever.

On Christmas Day 1942 we left for Gibraltar for minor repairs. German propaganda reports had us badly damaged. As we left Algiers we heard that the French admiral, Darlan had been shot — not surprising really as no one knew for sure whose side he was on anyway. Nor did he for that matter. It was said that one of our ship's company had written home to say someone had made a good job with Darlan, but the trouble was they shot the wrong admiral — meaning, of course, our own C.-in-C., for, despite what was reported in the home press, Admiral A. B. Cunningham was far from popular. To us it seemed strange that after a visit or a conference, particularly in Casablanca, inevitably a heavy air raid on the meeting place followed; Algiers received an especially heavy one. *Dido* was there at the time. This raid was widely reported in the home press. Incidentally, Algiers had very poor AA defence while Admiral Cunningham was there.

1943 — On January 9th, the damaged propeller having been changed, we moved to Bone, remaining there until the 29th, during which time the harbour suffered five days and four nights of air raids. The daytime raids were by fighters, which provided some near misses, particularly once when we were shifting berths, but we sustained no damage or casualties. We moved back to Algiers on the 29th, and there was an evening raid the following day.

Penelope joined the squadron on February 3rd. We moved back to Bone on the 13th with *Aurora*. On the 17th the Americans were driven some miles back into Tunisia — giving Rommel elbow room to counter the 8th Army threat from Tripoli. There were now fewer air raids and we had only one day raid and one dawn raid before returning to Algiers, arriving on the 23rd.

On Sunday, March 7th we were visited by the C.-in-C. (Admiral Cunningham) to inspect and address the ship's company. It was a miserable, damp morning and he arrived three quarters of an hour late, which didn't help the mood of the ship's company, who were by that time very restless indeed. Admiral Cunnigham began his address: "Well, *Dido*, I am very pleased to have you under my command."

"Well, we ain't," called a sailor.

"You have had the fleshpots of the USA. (No mention of his own recent year in the USA, or that some of the ship's company had left, to be replaced by others who had been away longer than we had, and had never seen New York.) You have enjoyed the fleshpots of Malta and Alexandria, such as they are. It is now time to get down to serious business. Owing to the evacuation of Tunisia I cannot afford to release any ships from the fleet. (More rumblings from the men.) I intend to use destroyers by day and cruisers by night — never mind those little birds that fly up above (waving his hands in the air)."

"Well, why don't you come out and join us then?" (Referring to the fact that the admiral rarely went to sea.)

I use the polite version of the last remark made by a sailor. The remark obviously angered the admiral as he stormed off the ship without the usual formalities.

On the 9th Algiers was ineffectively raided at dusk. Nevertheless, while the raid was in progress the order was given, 'Attention on the upper deck! Hands face aft!' Yes! The order had been given for 'Colours'. We must follow routine, come what may. We remained at Algiers until the 14th. On the way to Bone, in company with *Aurora*, *Laforey* and *Lookout*, we were attacked about fifty miles north-west of the port by eight low-flying Heinkels. Fortunately we had just contacted our first flight escort of the day and put them straight on to the enemy. Two were shot down and the rest dropped their torpedoes well out of range as they fled. On the 24th we returned to Algiers, having had a raid-free stay at Bone. On the 26th twelve low-flying aircraft raided Algiers at dusk, dropping circling torpedoes. One of these failed to explode, was made safe next morning, and brought aboard *Dido* to pacify our torpedo officer who had previously won the George Cross for playing with such unattractive weapons.

On April 4th, CS 12 Rear Admiral Harcourt inspected divisions and spoke to the ship's company. We continued at Algiers until returning to Bone and another night raid — more noisy than dangerous. On the 16th we returned to Algiers, having trouble with shadowers en route. This merely improved the good news that we were to go home to modernise our radio direction-finding equipment and give a spell of well-earned leave to the ship's crew. Most of us had not seen our homes for well over two years, after going through Atlantic convoys, Crete, Mediterranean convoys, etc., etc., and we were ready for a long break. It was two and a half years since I personally had seen my home.

We left Algiers for England on the 17th. At first we were told we were going to Newcastle, and arrangements were made for four weeks' leave to be spread over six weeks and three watches: (a) One watch the first four weeks; (b) One watch the last four weeks; and (c) One watch the first two and last two weeks. I was given (c) and was not very happy, as I had endured the journey from Newcastle to Liverpool my last time home. However, after leaving Gibraltar we were told we were going to Gladstone Dock in Liverpool, which for me (except for a few 'duty' days) meant six weeks' leave. How lucky can you be? During our stay in England we were to meet and greet the people of Bolton (who had adopted *Dido* as their ship) and exchange gifts etc., beginning a firm friendship which was to last a great many years and is still ongoing, including receiving the honour of the Freedom of Bolton for the ship and her company.

We spent May at Cammel Laird's and Gladstone Dock.

On June 14th we sailed for Scapa Flow for a short work-up (only 150 of the ship's company having been changed), returning to Liverpool on the 21st for completion of certain electrical work. On the 24th we sailed for the Mediterranean, reaching Gibraltar on the 24th — a main steam burst in the engine room, happily not causing any casualties. Our own engine-room staff completed successful repairs under very difficult conditions — then we travelled on to Algiers, arriving on the 28th. In our absence North Africa had been entirely cleared of the enemy, but we had missed nothing, as there had been no work for cruisers to do.

On July 2nd we arrived at Bone and again joined *Sirius*. On the 5th we moved to Bizerta (the captain's cat giving birth to five kittens en route), where in the early hours of the 6th there was an air raid — then back to Bone on the 7th. On the 10th the Sicilian Campaign started with added landings on the south-east corner. Though the other cruisers of the 12th and 15th squadrons were in support of the army, the role of *Dido* and *Sirius* was the less exciting one of being in reserve with *Howe* and *King George V.* We sailed that day, meeting the battleships at sea, spending the night in their company, and returning to Bone for a few hours on the 11th. At noon we sailed again to rejoin *Howe* and *King George V* and set out to create a diversion off the north-west corner of Sicily. The battleships bombarded Trapani, and the cruisers Marsala, from 21,000 yards. This was intended to simulate a further landing and was, I believe, successful in preventing troops from that area being released to join the main battle. We remained at Bone for the rest of the month, except for one hurried exit on the 14th when the Littorios (a class of Italian battleship) were reported to have left Spezia, and on the 27th when we sailed to escort *Indomitable* (damaged by torpedo) through the Sicilian Channel.

Having sailed with *Sirius* and two destroyers on the 31st July, we bombarded the bridge over the Olivia River in the early hours of August 1st. This was designed to interrupt enemy rail communications up the west coast of Italy. This shoot was carried out at 6,000 yards using star shells. The defence smoke put up by the enemy made observation difficult, but some shells were seen to hit the bridge. We returned to Bone later that day and moved with *Sirius* to Bizerta on the 3rd. While securing ship in the avant-ports, most of our weed traps became choked with seaweed, which lay six feet deep on the harbour floor. On the 7th there was an early-morning air raid and on the 9th and 10th we were at sea for a sweep with the rest of the squadron — with no result.

We sailed again on the 14th with *Sirius* and the two destroyers to bombard Scalea on the west coast of Italy at close range on the 15th. A German Army HQ was supposed to be located there. The force returned to Palermo, sailing again in the afternoon of the 15th and doing a sweep down the west coast of Italy, during which we sank three small enemy craft and bombarded the harbour of Vibo Valentia, which had been shot up a few days before by *Aurora* and *Penelope*. We returned to Bizerta in the afternoon of the 16th, and on the 17th enjoyed a fairly extended stay, which found all the cruisers' captains ashore — lunching with the flag officers. On the 18th we sailed with *Aurora* and two destroyers and sunk ten enemy craft just north of Scalea. They were evacuating men and ammunition (judging by the way some of them exploded). We then continued northward because of the army's landings in the toe of Italy. A sweep the next night with *Sirius* found nothing and ended this particular phase of naval activity. On the 20th we returned to Bizerta, passing through the partially blocked canal and on north-west with *Sirius* to Palermo, by now in efficient US occupation. It was a considerable while since we had enjoyed shore time and we were glad of a break in Palermo.

In the early days of September occasional aircraft arrived at Palermo, starting rumours of an Italian armistice.

On the 7th, at Bizerta, we embarked 612 airborne troops and forty tons of their weapons and stores. (As I passed the POs' mess, I noticed that on top of the stack of the sergeants' kit outside was one belonging to a pre-war friend. I had a chat with him before he left the ship and I haven't seen him since.) The Italians *had* capitulated. *Aurora* (CS12), *Penelope*, *Sirius*, *Dido*, *Abdiel* (later sunk by a mine in harbour) and USS *Boise* having all embarked troops, sailed on the afternoon of the 8th for Taranto to accept the surrender of the Italian fleet, being joined at sea by *Howe* and *King George V* under the command of Vice Admiral A. J. Power. As we approached Taranto on the 9th, with our minesweepers getting into position ahead, two Italian battleships and two cruisers could be seen leaving the harbour on their way to Malta and surrender.

The whole force, apart from *King George V*, entered Taranto at dusk and anchored in the Mare Grano. Our intended anchor berth was inaccessible, so we secured to buoys inside an anti-torpedo net, a berth that had just recently been occupied by one of the Italian cruisers. The work of unloading the troops and equipment proceeded swiftly and by the next morning they had advanced well toward Bari and had secured Taranto undamaged and ready for subsequent use.

At midnight (9th/10th) *Abdiel* blew up at anchor and sank in a minute and a half. She had swung over a magnetic mine, thirty of which, it was subsequently learned, German U-boats had surreptitiously laid by night, before evacuating Taranto. It was fortunate that no other ships were lost, as nearly twenty of these mines were exploded by our own minesweepers on the 10th. We had all passed over several. In the early hours of the 10th the force sailed for Bizerta, where the British cruisers embarked more troops and stores (*Dido* took 393 airborne troops and eighty tons of stores, including eight jeeps, eight trailers, fourteen motorcycles and eight six-pounder guns). The 12th Cruiser Squadron sailed for Taranto, arriving on the 12th, anchoring this time outside the harbour, and discharging men and stores during the night. On the 13th, *Aurora* and *Penelope* left for Salerno to reinforce the bombarding squadron supporting the landing there. On the 14th *Dido* and *Sirius* left for Augusta.

The situation of the British/American forces ashore at Salerno (which operation was later to be named 'Avalanches') had become precarious, so on the 16th *Dido* and *Sirius* were sent to join the bombarding squadron, arriving on the 17th. From then until the 25th we were engaged in a total of thirty very successful bombardments of the Italian coast, in support of the army at Salerno, including eleven counter-battery shoots and eight shoots against motor transport and tanks. During this period the German counter-attacks were brought to a halt and our own troops attacked and advanced until they were out of range of our guns. All shoots were carried out while at anchor — mostly off the lovely town of Amalfi. On the 17th, 18th and 21st, enemy shells fell close while we were near the main anchorage. On the 17th there was a rocket-bomb attack from 24,000 ft; our AA fire went very close to the aircraft, and that was the last attack. On the 18th there were two small fighter-bomber attacks, in the second of which we were straddled by their bombs. Yes! The gunners deserved the many accolades they received for destroying targets including, as requested by General Alexander, the destruction of the hillside, thereby blocking the main highway from Naples to Rome and cutting off one avenue of retreat. In addition every target, including tanks was actually hit. On September 28th we left for Malta, and on arrival we secured in the Grand Harbour. A great change for the better had taken place since we were last there in December 1942, except that the dockyard was on strike, so that all loading of ammunition, stores and provisions had to be carried out by our own working parties.

In October, following the Italian surrender, the Aegean islands of Samos, Leros, Kos and Kalymaos had been occupied by British troops — Rhodes remaining in German hands. The Germans were taking steps to oust our troops from the Aegean, so on October 3rd *Aurora* and *Penelope* were ordered to Alexandria, followed on 4th by *Sirius* and *Dido*. Early on the 5th we were ordered to join *Aurora* and two destroyers, ready to do a sweep east of the island. Unfortunately, when joining up with *Aurora* in the moonlight, both ships doing 28 knots, Captain Terry made a bad error of judgement, so that we formed alongside instead of astern of *Aurora*. Although Captain Terry himself took responsibility, the rear admiral in *Aurora* blamed our camouflage — at the time a multicoloured cloud effect — painted during our refit in Birkenhead. The result was that *Aurora*'s anchor was stuck in our port bow.

We had to go to Alexandria for repairs and also change our colours to those of the Med fleet. On such occasions it was the practice for the captain to send for the engine-room registers to check if we had 'obeyed telegraphs at all times'. We had, of course, as the commander (E) told him in no uncertain terms before he would release the registers. It was usual for the engine room to be blamed for incidents such as the *Aurora* collision, as the commander was well aware, so he was always prepared if anything happened. We remained in Alex for five weeks while other tragedies were taking place in the Dodecanese. After temporary repairs had been carried out in Alexandria, the C.-in-C. ordered permanent repairs including repainting the camouflage in Mediterranean colours. In this we were perhaps lucky, as during the past few weeks *Aurora*, *Sirius*, *Penelope* and *Carlisle* all received severe bomb damage and casualties. Seven destroyers were lost and the Germans regained all the captured islands. When we were ready to leave Alexandria these episodes had ceased — another lucky escape. Repairs completed, we returned to Malta. Later, we spent Christmas in Taranto — not the best place to spend Christmas.

1944 — In January, the army, after successfully advancing from the toe of Italy and negotiating Salerno, had become stuck south of Formia; and a landing was carried out at Anzio, with the object of cutting the enemy's communications and forcing him to withdraw. During this operation we had an unusual assignment. We carried all kinds of small metal plates attached to a barrage balloon covered with tinfoil. In company with a number of MTBs we sailed for Civitavecchia to create a diversionary landing during the main landings at Anzio. The idea, of course, was that the enemy would pick up 'signals' from the balloon and our escorts, being led to believe another invasion was in progress. The C.-in-C. later told us that our diversion had been a complete success.

On securing to the oiler on our return to Naples at 12.30 on the 22nd, the captain was ordered by the C.-in-C. to take *Le Fantasque* (a French destroyer), *Inglefield* and *Kempenfelt* to the Gulf of Gaeta, and block the road at Terracina and Formia, to prevent German troops being moved north to Anzio. The destroyers went to Formia, while we concentrated on the road at Terracina, carrying out several shoots between 16.30 on the 22nd and 07.10 on the 23rd. At 14.00 on the 23rd, we also shot up a shore battery which had been annoying the destroyers. The captain received a private message of thanks from General Alexander for having achieved our objectives. The force was then recalled to Naples.

At noon on the 25th we sailed again for the Gulf of Gaeta, registered visually on Gaeta Point (the weather being too bad for air observation), and that night carried out five area shoots, designed to interfere with the movement of enemy troops and supplies. During the afternoon of the 26th we carried out our first shoot using an air-to-air OP, interrupting it to shoot up the battery on Gaeta Point, which had the temerity to open fire on us. At 21.05 one more shoot was carried out and we returned to Naples. We left again early on the 28th, taking Admiral Sir John Cunningham and his staff to Anzio. No supporting fire was required that day, but we remained in the area, watching several air raids on the port, through the day and night. Next day, the 29th, we started supporting US minesweepers, extending the swept channel to the north; then moved to the southern (US) sector, carrying out three bombardments. Just after anchoring at dusk, we suffered a glider-bomb attack by about ten aircraft.

Two of these hit merchant ships, and one hit *Spartan* at 17.55, causing a bad fire and allowing water to enter the ship, beyond control. At 19.05 she capsized and later sank. Unfortunately, her damage-control organisation was not as efficient as it should have been, and at a subsequent inquiry many new regulations and instructions were issued regarding damage-control efficiency. *Dido* embarked 284 survivors, *Delhi* the remainder.

We sailed at 22.15. We had been delayed, waiting for our motor cutter, which had broken down; but had to leave as a further air raid developed. As we left via the swept channel at 25 knots, flares fell ahead and astern of us, followed by a stick of four bombs, luckily one cable (six feet) from our port quarter. We secured in Naples Harbour at 05.00 on the 30th without further incident.

On February 2nd we were again at Anzio and carried out two bombardments. An enemy battery took some interest in us — one of their salvos straddling — no damage.

Next morning we were back at Naples; several days of rough weather followed.

On the 7th we were giving leave at Torre Annunziata when we were ordered to Formia to join *Penelope*, supporting a projected army attack, but on reaching the area we came under accurate fire and had to desist. However, the army's party was cancelled and we returned to Naples.

On the 12th we proceeded to Formia with a smoke-laying ML, and in spite of being under fire most of the day — with one or two shots landing no more than twenty-five yards away — we carried out seven day shoots, two of them registering on night targets, and three night harassing shoots on the enemy's lines of communication.

On the 17th we carried out six bombardments at Anzio without interference, using American fighter-spotting for the first time. Just after dusk in Naples Bay, we had the misfortune to collide with an American LCI, which elected to change course across our bow (apparently without seeing our navigation light) when it was too late to avoid a collision. He was undamaged, but tore a large hole in our starboard side abreast of B turret, sadly killing four men and injuring four more who recovered later. But for the judgement of Captain Terry it might have been worse.

The following morning we should have relieved another cruiser, *Penelope*, in the Gulf of Gaeta, but were unable to do so. As she steamed around waiting for us she was hit twice in a U-boat attack, first in the stern, then midships, and sank with the loss of 411 men, amongst whom, I later learned, were two of my friends. Although we were operating from Naples, we had to go to Malta and Alexandria for repairs and supplies, etc. Fortunately this marked the end of the bombardment season, so our absence had no serious effect.

These operations off south-west Italy needed extra vigilance, mainly because of the volcanic island of Stromboli; the light from whose continuous eruptions illuminated shipping at night, making easy prey for lurking U-boats and E-boats. If anything, the bombardments had improved the bond between Captain Terry and his ship's company. For instance, prior to one bombardment, a voice boomed through the loudspeakers, "This is your captain speaking, there has been too much loafing around the upper deck during these shoots. If I see anyone, I'll come down and wring his b . . . y neck." Result — decks were kept clear.

After a quiet month being repaired, we sailed on March 30th for exercises, returning to Malta Grand Harbour on April 2nd.

On April 4th we arrived at Naples and remained there with *Ajax* and *Sirius* in case of a call for bombardment.

On the 21st Rear Admiral J. M. Mansfield hoisted his flag aboard as C.-in-C. Cruiser Squadron 15. About this time *Orion*, *Ajax* and *Sirius* left for the UK to form part of the bombardment for the invasion of Europe, leaving *Dido* as the sole British cruiser operative in the Mediterranean. Naples Harbour was raided on April 24th.

It was part of the Allied plan that the Italian offensive should start on May 11th — object Rome — and as far north as possible. General Mark Clark paid tribute to the share of the naval forces in the triumph. With *Dido,* ready to bombard, were USS *Philadelphia* (Rear Admiral Davidson), USS *Brooklyn* and six US destroyers. Two US destroyers, *Mackenzie* and *Ordronaux*, had been allocated to us as screen, so we sailed with them on May 12th to the Gulf of Gaeta to 'open the ball'. Three shoots were carried out that day, two at gun positions and one at our old friend Terracina.

On the 15th we were again in the area and carried out nine shoots at targets in the Itri-Gaeta area, also at Terracina and Sperlonga. Opposition from a shore battery proved ineffective.

By May 18th we were again in the area. The army had progressed so well that the zone of possible targets was severely limited. However, we did manage to shoot successfully at five without experiencing any effective opposition.

Shortly after anchoring off Sorrento, one of the stop valves on B2 boiler suddenly disintegrated, due to old age and constant use. This necessitated dockyard treatment, so on the 19th we sailed for Malta with USS *Mackenzie* and *Ordronaux*, arriving on May 20th.

On June 2nd we returned to Naples to continue our tasks with *Mackenzie* and *Ordronaux*, and to carry out sporadic bombardments of Italy.

On the 4th, the day our troops entered Rome, we went to Anzio in the hope of getting some shooting. However, there was nothing doing and we returned to Naples.

On the 6th the great landing took place in Normandy. Though we could not be there, we had helped by what we did here in May.

On the 17th we went to Malta, exercising at sea on the 27th, then returned to Naples.

Meanwhile, it was around this time that Captain Terry announced some awards made to the ship for the Anzio Campaign. To my amazement, and the astonishment of my messmates, I had been awarded a mention in dispatches. It was some time before I knew why. Apparently our commander (E) had been looking through my confidential service records and noticed that my actions at Crete had not been recognised by his predecessor. As I was told this in confidence, I never told my messmates the truth. By this time most of the ERAs at Crete had left the ship and had been replaced.

On July 24th HM the King reviewed the fleet in Naples Bay, then we crossed over to Propriano in Corsica to prepare for the landings in Southern France. When we left in August we could hardly see the sea for ships of all shapes and sizes, or the sky for aircraft — a mighty armada. The Rt Hon Winston Churchill passed through those lines of ships in a destroyer. In company with the French cruiser *Gloire* and a sloop carrying French, American and British commandos we went ahead. After we bombarded the coast, the troops landed and it was all over in a short while.

The following morning the fleet arrived flying their battle ensigns — 'Do you mind if we join your private war?' It was all finished by then, but I believe they fired a few rounds just to show their presence.

After this the other ships returned to home waters, but we stayed for a while as the only RN cruiser in the Mediterranean, in company with the USS *Ordronaux* and *McKenzie*. We were kept busy occasionally shelling the Italian coast.

It was September 3rd when we finally left the Med to return to the Home fleet. In the last three and a half years we had experienced many emotions — greatness, sadness, happiness, gloom, frustration, excitement. There were fearless and fearful times, but we came through it all, having lost good pals and found new ones.

It would seem that at times we were on a Cook's tour, visiting so many exotic places. Not so! For in our early years we 'junior' ERAs had to use much of our off-duty time studying on courses, and sitting exams to gain advancement. Until these were completed leave was restricted.

So what was in store for us in the Home fleet? Firstly there was leave, during which many of us were happy to complete other commitments, including myself getting married.

After this our first operation was a convoy (yet again) but this time Russian. It was quite a contrast to the Mediterranean, as, apart from the atrocious weather, during which the seamen were kept busy chipping ice off the deck, etc., there were no problems — no hostile aircraft, submarines or surface craft. On our return we again had a new captain — Captain R. F. Elkins, of whom we knew nothing until he told us his story at a later date.

HMS Dido *in the Mediterranean, August 1944*

HMS Dido in the Arctic, October 1944

Captain R. F. Elkins RN

CHAPTER 3

THIRD COMMISSION
November 1944 - January 1946

The time between November 1944 and April 1945 was taken up with supporting air strikes off Norway. At times the weather was so bad that some ships were damaged by heavy seas and were recalled to base, but we had to struggle on, wondering what we had done to deserve such punishment, though at Christmas we managed some leave which had been owing to us.

By April we were back in the Arctic, this time escorting the minelaying cruiser *Apollo* and two minelaying destroyers, *Obdurate* and *Obedient* around the North Cape and the Kola Inlet where we were to see the Russian battleship *Archangelsk* (formerly HMS *Royal Sovereign*, now on Lend-Lease to Russia). She was lying at anchor in Murmansk, never put to sea, and was only returned to Britain long after the agreed date. The reason for the operation was that the main convoys to Russia had ceased, but U-boats were picking off single ships in that area, and sinking them with ease. The Russians refused to help with laying an anti-submarine minefield, so we laid it ourselves, whether they liked it or not. The guns were not required for this trip, but naturally the engines were. Most of the way there and back we travelled at high speed — engine power needed here. On our return we were addressed by an admiral of the cruiser squadron, who told us why we had sailed at high speed. It seemed that no less than thirty-six submarines had been in the area, waiting for us, but couldn't catch us. By this time the war in Europe was almost over and we went to Rosyth for much-needed rest and leave.

The plan was to give leave to 50% of the ship's company and, on their return, the rest would be given leave. Once again plans were to go awry. I was on leave and visiting friends and on returning home at 1.00 a.m. a telegram awaited me — 'Report on board forthwith'! So with very little sleep that night it was back to the ship from Liverpool. Captain Elkins was very concerned about this recall. I was told he was very annoyed at *Dido*'s recall when there were so many other ships in the Firth of Forth, doing nothing. He vowed that on our return he would visit the C.-in-C. to demand an explanation and make sure all leave passes and travel warrants would be cancelled to start afresh. He did just that and off we went for our ten days. The rest had fifteen days (only ten officially). Yes! That was the extent of Captain Elkins' regard for his men.

But why were we recalled? It was the end of April, the war was almost over and no aircraft in sight. However, at 5.00 p.m. on Sunday we sailed, not knowing where until the captain spoke to us and told us we were about to meet other ships off Norway to decide who should go to Norway and who to Copenhagen. In company with HMS *Birmingham* (carrying the senior officer) and four Z-class destroyers we were sent to Copenhagen — passing through the Skagerrak and the Kattegat, and including a minefield on the way. A mine stuck in *Birmingham*'s paravane chains, which are supposed to keep mines away from ships. Fortunately it did not explode. The riflemen on both ships, including Captain Elkins, had a great time taking potshots at mines, but had to be careful not to explode any. *Dido* then went ahead as the leader of the group. It was now VE day, the army had finished fighting and the air force flying, but the navy had to carry on until midnight. At about 10.00 p.m. a German aircraft approached without giving recognition signals, so we fired one shot at it — missed, of course. That shot was the last one fired in the war in Europe.

Copenhagen, then, was to be our great reward. In the dockyard lay the German cruisers *Prinz Eugen* and *Nurnberg* and other smaller ships. Also there were hundreds of German soldiers. The German Navy was about to surrender. Some of the smaller ships, not happy about this, objected and had to be somewhat restrained. Worse than that, it interrupted our shore leave. After many toings and froings the surrender of the German Navy was duly signed aboard HMS *Dido*. We returned to peacetime Britain to resume our interrupted leave, though the war was not yet over in the Far East. En route we escorted *Prinz Eugen* and *Nurnberg* to Kiel Harbour.

Captain Elkins spoke fluent German; perhaps this was the reason

Delivering the surrender terms aboard the German cruiser Prinz Eugen

German Kriegsmarine officers arriving aboard
HMS Dido *to sign the surrender*

for *our* recall — he was able to discuss the surrender terms with the German naval officers. We also had a visit from Field Marshal Montgomery — not particularly exciting. I cannot praise the Danish people enough for their hospitality. I still correspond with friends I made there and have since paid a visit to them, once again to be made very welcome.

The best was yet to come, for in July 1945 we conveyed Their Majesties King George VI and Queen Elizabeth to the Isle of Man for a four-day visit. Wearing the royal standard at our masthead made that time the proudest of our lives.

It was foggy all through the four days — Bolton Holiday Week. I later learned that, according to Manx folklore, whenever a foreign monarch visited the island, on the orders of King Manannan (a sort of Manx Neptune) it would be shrouded in mist. Strange, but seemingly true, as the fog lifted the moment we left.

Now a word about Captain Elkins, who was a great man in every respect. Early in 1940, as a commander, he was sent, along with an army colonel, to organise the withdrawal of the 51st Division at St Valery, but their plans went awry and they found themselves on the St Valery beach. Captain Elkins was a champion 'Bisley' shot, and from the shelter of some rocks he fired his rifle at a German staff car. The shot went over the top of the car — he said that in his excitement he forgot to set the sights properly. The occupant of the car was no other than General (later Field Marshal) Rommel. One wonders what course the war would have taken if the shot had hit its target. However, the captain was taken prisoner and later escaped, but that is another story.

When he was appointed to the ship he had told us he was to take us for an extended refit and then on to join the Pacific fleet, but it was not to be, for the Japanese surrendered. I often jokingly wondered if, in addition to the two A-bombs, the Japanese high command had heard that *Dido* was on the way, although they had been led to believe she had been sunk — a ghost ship perhaps. After all, we had seen the surrender of the Italians in Assab, the surrender of the Italian navy at Taranto, told the Russians what to do with their navy, and received the surrender of the German Navy in Copenhagen. Is it any wonder the Japanese surrendered unconditionally?

Now what about the engine-room/gunnery-department rivalry? The gunnery, whether ack-ack in keeping aircraft away (as at Crete,) in surface action (such as at Sirte), and in many bombardments (in North Africa and Italy), was excellent. Sometimes they ran out of ammunition; sometimes we had to go into a dockyard to replace gun barrels as they wore out. All praise to them! But how did they manage to get to all the different destinations in all kinds of weather, be it in the heat and comparative calm of the Mediterranean or the mountainous seas and ice of the Arctic, high speed or slow, as required — our 4 HP turbines never failed us. I think that's all I need to say on this subject.

The next few months on the ship were an anticlimax and rather dull, apart from a visit to the ship in the Firth of Forth by Their Majesties the King and Queen. However, at 8.00 a.m. on January 10th 1946 I left the ship and the navy. Captain Elkins himself wished me luck and thanked me for my services to the ship. He later rose to the rank of admiral and received a knighthood.

On reflection, life on the ship, though hard and dangerous at times, had its lighter moments. What would a ship be without its characters and their antics aboard and ashore? A ship's company makes the ship and *Dido*'s had all the qualities needed for a clean, happy and efficient ship.

Yes! Perhaps it could be said that *Dido* was a lucky ship, but on reflection I know not why or how, given the number of near misses we had from bombs, torpedoes, shells and even mines. At times even the heavy weather was in our favour. The extraordinary exchanges of position in convoys, and even two fairly light collisions (both at dusk and in uncertain weather), though regrettably causing casualties and loss of life, saved us from more serious action and possibly disaster. Although the vicious weather in the Atlantic and Arctic Oceans and the North Sea meant that instead of good solid meals we had to live on soup, ship's biscuits, and corned-beef sandwiches for weeks on end, it saved us from submarine, surface and air attacks. In fact, on the Russian convoy, while I was on watch in the after engine room, there was such a huge crash on the ship's side and water came pouring in through the ventilators, half flooding the engine room to such an extent we thought we had been torpedoed, but an extra large wave had passed over us — some sea! With all this in mind, I have often thought the Royal Naval Prayer should be slightly amended — 'O Eternal Lord God, who alone spreadest out the heavens and rulest the raging of the sea; who has compassed the waters with bounds until day and night come to an end . . . Preserve us from the *dangers* of the sea, and from the *violence* of the enemy . . .' Maybe it should be changed to 'the *violence* of the sea and from the *dangers* of the enemy'!

One evening, when I was in charge of the engineers' workshop, the warrant electrical officer asked my permission to use a lathe. Following our conversation we became firm friends, although officer/rating fraternisation was not encouraged in the Royal Navy. When in harbour we used to attend church together, though we were not allowed to leave the ship together. Ashore we were Bill and Eric — on board it was Sir and Chief. This was how it had to be, it was recognised by all concerned, and I believe it should still be so. (This protocol also affected inter-rating relationships. In New York I was refused a special weekend leave as I was going with ratings junior to me — two seamen and a stoker — while I was about to be upgraded to petty officer.) Bill shared a cabin with a warrant engineer who, when he himself was ashore on Sunday evenings in harbour, graciously allowed Bill to use the cabin for what we called a 'Cabin Fellowship', sometimes cramming about twelve into the small cabin for a Bible reading, prayer fellowship and a general natter. This became an invaluable half-hour or so to us all, even earning the respect of some of the ship's company. Incidentally, it was Bill who told me of a conversation he had with the commander (E) about my award. Yes, we were a lucky ship, but was it all luck? I am not too sure. Perhaps I was a talisman!

Although her crew received many personal awards — DSO (Captain McCall), DSCs, DSMs, and mentions in dispatches — *Dido* was not given the praise, plaudits and publicity afforded to other ships; for instance, the Battles of Sirte and El Alamein, operations in Southern France, the surrender of the German Navy at Copenhagen, etc. I searched for many years before I found a publication which gave the ship due credit — that epitome of the 'Silent Service', a book entitled *Battleships, Cruisers and Destroyers*.

PART II

Ashore and Afloat

Like most ships in World War II, *Dido* was overmanned, carrying a ship's company in excess of her designed complement. The chief and ERA's mess was no exception. In fact the chief and PO's recreation space had to be used as an overflow mess for the junior ERAs over-complement. It was most uncomfortable at night or in bad weather at sea, when all portholes had to be closed. The ventilation wasn't very efficient and, especially with so many smokers, the atmosphere became very unpleasant. There were times when it was preferable to be on watch in the engine room or boiler room. Following a spell of a week or so it was a relief to return to a bleak Scapa Flow for an hour or so ashore and some fresh air, though at times it could be too fresh. Matters weren't improved much in the Med and it was even worse in the Red Sea. At least we could spend more time on deck when not on watch or battened down at action stations, as we were most of the time when at sea. In addition we junior ERAs had to take advancement courses (sometimes in off-duty hours) so we took every opportunity for shore leave.

So what did we do ashore? In bleak Scapa Flow not much except for sport, cinema and, most importantly, there was the canteen where we could eat a meal in comfort without having to chase it across the table, as we had to do at sea.

For most of us Freetown was our first time ashore in foreign parts, especially in the tropics. We had been issued with tropical kit. Thus dressed some of the ship's company resembled nothing so much as characters from a comic opera. There were so many shapes and sizes — shorter men with their white shorts down to the

44

knees (some even lower); taller men whose shorts just about covered their requirements. There were belts meeting with difficulty, and others so long as not to fasten closely enough, while just about holding up. The port was not very impressive, but at least there was fresh fruit. Much of our spare space was taken up by fruit unobtainable at home.

Then it was back to the trials and tribulations of Atlantic convoys, followed by Christmas leave at home — sadly the last for some time, in my case for two and a half years. More treacherous Atlantic convoys were to follow before our return to the Mediterranean in April. At least in the daytime we could let some fresh air into a mess normally full of tobacco smoke and stale air through open portholes fitted with wind scoops. Nights were unbearable, owing to the so-called air conditioning not being very efficient and 'Darken Ship' (no portholes open). We had to put up with it, though it did not contribute to the sweetness of temper of the crew. As far as I was concerned sightseeing was a priority. Many of the ship's company, including some messmates, never went beyond the local bars or other attractions. Happily this was not my idea of entertainment, even in New York. Fortunately this period did not last too long, though unfortunately it was followed by the disaster at Crete.

After Crete, in early June, we left Alexandria for our first journey through the Suez Canal, the first stop being Port Tewfik to remove some debris, and also to collect mail salvaged from a damaged troopship — then on to Mombassa for some shore leave. Unfortunately, on the way back to the ship I stumbled. I cannot recall how or why, but it was certainly not alcohol-related. It resulted in a few days confined to the sickbay, by which time Germany had invaded Russia. From Alexandria we had on board the French equivalent of an ERA who became most indignant and annoyed when he was told he had to work his passage. However, he left us at our next stop — Durban — where we stayed about three weeks for temporary repairs to be made more permanent.

The remains of B turret were completely removed and the deck concreted over. What a delight to see a city so bright and cheerful with plenty of good, wholesome food. A particular few of us spent a few days in Pietermaritzburg. Then we were on our way to Simonstown (for Cape Town) for tests in dry dock. One celebrity, a dog called Nuisance, knew the times of the trains the sailors and dockyard workers used between Simonstown and Cape Town. She even had her own rail season ticket and became a national pet. When she died a monument was erected to her. We left Durban still not knowing our final destination, making a short stop at St Helena for oil — no shore leave here. It was then we heard we were headed for Brooklyn Navy Yard, New York after a weekend in Port of Spain, Trinidad. During this trip we met USS *Omaha* who challenged us, not knowing who we were, though we knew who she was, as we had RDF (radio direction-finders) and *Omaha* had not. We heard later that several of her ship's company were disciplined.

We had a wonderful time in America. After a short trial period we were accepted as friends. Most places of leisure — cinemas, theatres, bars, etc. — were free or subject only to a few cents entertainment tax. On one occasion I enjoyed a production of *Macbeth*, starring world-renowned actors Maurice Evans and Judith Anderson in the leading roles, though to me it was a little irksome to hear 'dollars', instead of 'crowns', and other Americanisms. I also saw many other great films and plays of that era, returning well after midnight after going from one to another. An organisation named the British War Relief Society in New York arranged a great amount of hospitality for us, including even the famous RCA Music Hall. Some of us were lucky enough to be invited to stay in private homes at weekends, which was just as well as our pay, unlike that of the US forces, did not stretch very far. A few were even more fortunate as they had relatives or friends not far away. It may be of interest here to note that one day when the ship's stores were being replenished I noticed a carcass of meat being loaded, stamped 'Rejected by the USN — Unfit for consumption'. So much for Lend-Lease — but we came to no harm.

On completion of the refit we exercised off Rhode Island, returning to the navy yard for adjustments and some engine repairs. We finally left New York for exercises off Bermuda just a few days before Pearl Harbor and America's entry into the war.

On our return to the Med from New York our base for a while was Alexandria. Although we spent a great deal of time at sea we did have shore leave one night in three, which followed the most popular pattern. This was the time of bombardment along the North African coast, Malta convoys, and the Battle of Sirte. Then we were forced out of Alexandria to take up residence in Haifa or Port Said. The Mediterranean was of course a golden opportunity to see some ancient places and improve our knowledge of history, geography and religion. I learned more about these in a few visits than I did in all my years at school.

While at Haifa — then in Palestine — we had plenty of shore leave, so used the opportunity to take part in organised trips to Jerusalem, Bethlehem, Galilee, the Dead Sea and Nazareth. We travelled in two buses — one with an Arab driver, the other Jewish. They had to use different routes and avoid each other's territory, but arrived at our destination at the same time, even allowing for our bus breaking down about a dozen times. The visit to the Holy Land was of special interest to me, as I wanted to further my knowledge of Biblical history and its meaning for life. One incident in Jerusalem was amusing — it cost one shilling to become a pilgrim and two shillings to become a knight pilgrim. A member of our party paid his two shillings to be a knight pilgrim — and he was a Jew!

We did get one run to Malta, at the end of the siege when, for a while, the Eastern Med had quietened down a little. We then saw how the island had suffered — so many buildings destroyed and the people almost starving. The best we could get was cocoa without milk or sugar and a small snack. On leaving, the cruisers left three quarters of their stores and the destroyers most of theirs, keeping just enough to last until their return to base. Sometime later when we called again it was a somewhat different story. We could get almost anything we wanted — at a price — "Psst! Would you like an omelette?" — and beer was at an inflated price. Everything came from our own stores, sold back to us at exorbitant rates. Even the charge for the dhyso (ferry rowing boat) was ridiculous — so much so that one of our seamen was so annoyed he refused to pay, pushed the owner into the harbour and rowed back to the ship himself. The captain was not amused, nor was the sailor when he was punished accordingly.

We eventually returned to Port Said, going on later to a floating dock at Massawa in the Red Sea to carry out repairs. The temperature here was 135°F in the shade. In fact when we were working on deck our new commander (E) stopped the ship's butcher, who was carrying a block of ice for the officers' mess, and told him we were more important than the officers, who were not pleased at missing their cold drinks. This was to be the first of many altercations he won for the engineers over the seaman branch, including Captain Terry.

We were sent on three days' leave to Asmara in the hills of Eritrea, which was quite an experience — from 135°F at sea level to 40°F at 6,000ft. We were taken by army trucks along an Italian-designed road with 1,000 sharp hairpin bends. We were told that over 1,000 native lives were lost during its construction. These were three very pleasant days. Three of us hired bicycles for a day and travelled down this road for a couple of miles, then waited for an army truck. We would never have made it back up the steep road by pedal power.

Then it was back to Alexandria and the usual routine of exercises and bombardments of the North African coast, including the last at Tobruk. We were transferred to the Mediterranean fleet in time for the North African landings, and were based at Algiers, Bone and Bizerta to act as AA guard ship until our temporary return to the UK for a refit and HOME LEAVE — the first for two and a half years. During our absence North Africa had been entirely cleared of the enemy, but we had missed nothing, as there had been no work for the cruisers to do.

We arrived back in the Med in time for the Sicilian landings as AA support for the armies and extra bombardment, and to resume our role as AA guard ship at Algiers, etc., and then Palermo and Augusta. Apart from two hours at Palermo, shore leave was practically non-existent for some time, so much so that when the opportunity did come Captain Terry instructed the officers of the watch to be reasonably lenient with men returning on board. Of course there were some who overstepped the mark. One returned wearing just his boots and underwear. He said he had only drunk one bottle of Marsala wine — very potent at the best of times, made even worse by not having any alcohol to drink, apart from the daily rum tot, for some time.

Another, a messmate, returned on board with his boots unlaced, jacket unfastened, collar and tie on opposite sides of his neck and his cap on the back of his head — but worst of all one eye was closed.

The officer of the watch on duty at the time happened to be the most disliked officer on the ship. He greeted the lad with "Just look at you, you're an absolute disgrace. What's the matter with your eye?"

"Nothing, sir," was the reply. "It's here." And with that he produced a carefully folded clean handkerchief and opened it out to reveal a glass eye. The officer became the butt of jokes from the wardroom to the mess decks. Nevertheless, both these lads spent four days in the cells.

It was now September 1943. We went into Bizerta for boiler cleaning and some shore leave. Having started the boiler-clean, we had to replace our valves and equipment in a hurry and prepare for sea to embark the paras for Taranto. Alas — no shore leave!

From there it was round to Naples and the Salerno landings, then back to Malta for gun replacements, etc. As the Eastern Mediterranean area was hotting up again, we were diverted to meet *Aurora*. As explained earlier this was a calamity, though it was in some ways beneficial to the ship's company. Some took the chance of three days' leave in Cairo to see the Sphinx and Pyramids, ride a camel (somewhat akin to a boat on a choppy sea) and visit a cinema (departing flea-ridden). At the Pyramids we had our fortunes read in the sand, and were told, "You will go now and not return." (We did return to Alexandria later. Perhaps the fortune-teller, being Egyptian, hoped we might be eliminated by his Axis friends.)

When we were fit for sea duties it was back to Malta, and Taranto (Christmas 1943), then to take part in the landings at Anzio. Naples became our main base during these operations. The place was a disappointment — dirty and crime-ridden. The opera house, despite its appearance, was in use and we were able to see a production of *Madam Butterfly*, the heroine weighing at least twenty stone. We also saw the US production of Irving Berlin's *This is the Army*. Much to the annoyance of the US forces, the British NAAFI managed to get the best premises for their use. For security reasons when in Naples Bay the ships changed anchorages (shifted billets) in the evenings. Sometimes we were anchored off Sorrento, where three messmates and I went for a walk ashore. We were joined by a young boy who asked if we would like an orange. He climbed over a wall and returned with an orange big enough for four of us to share. We later discovered he had taken it from a convent orchard, but I understand no action was taken against him.

One afternoon I and three other engine-room chief POs arrived at the jetty at the correct time to return to the ship, but the coxswain of the liberty boat said "Sorry Chief, the boat's full, I'll have to come back for you with the officers' boat." We waited quite a long time before the boat arrived and were told, to our dismay, that we had been posted absent without leave. When we arrived back at the ship she was ready to sail. Much to the amusement of the seamen, four engine-room chief POs had to be hoisted on board in the boat. We were charged with being AWOL to appear the following morning as 'Commander's defaulters'. I (why me? I was the junior member of the quartet) explained to the commander what had happened. He sent for the coxswain, who verified my story, and the case was dismissed to the disappointment of the seamen, chiefs and POs. They had hoped we would get stoppage of leave. Another engine-room triumph over the seamen. A group of ERAs visited Puzzuoli and a nearby volcano, where a guide demonstrated his party piece by holding a piece of smoking paper over a small crack in the crater, causing smoke to rise from all the other cracks. He also explained that this was the burial place of Euryalus, who was in love with Dido, but she preferred the hunter Aeneas. The story had a tragic end, as illustrated by our ship's crest.

It was during one of these changing times that the US cruiser *Philadelphia* rammed and sank a US destroyer, *Bristol*. We later saw the full extent of the cruiser's badly damaged bows when she was in dry dock in Malta.

On another occasion our watch managed to get a morning run ashore at Pompeii, and when we arrived back on board the ship was ready for sea. Some U-boats were around the Gulf of Gaeta. We didn't find any and thankfully they didn't find us. We stayed at Naples for random bombardments along the Italian coast and prepared for the Southern France landings, before returning to home waters in September 1944.

Over the years most of the bases and ports we visited were of great interest, though some were not particularly so.

Alexandria, of course, was of great historical note; though we did not know then of the gold and treasures we 'sat on' from time to time. Naturally there were plenty of leisure palaces, for want of another name, for those who liked them, and an abundance of bars, cafés, cinemas, etc. A waiter in one café became used to me and always knew what I wanted. I spent a lot of my time at the Racing Club, improving my tennis in an effort to beat my brother on my return home — something I had never done before. Sadly he died at the age of twenty-nine, while I was away. There was always the sergeants' and chief POs' mess at the Fleet Club to enliven our spirits; and entertainment from ENSA stars such as George Formby. One Saturday morning while we were secured to a French cruiser, a young seaman, who was cleaning his machine gun, accidentally discharged the weapon and fired a bullet into a French officer's cabin. *Dido*'s Captain Terry made profuse apologies to the French officer and had a word for the seaman — "* * * * * *."

On one occasion I was able to visit my brother-in-law at Ras-el-Tin, the shore base. He was one of the survivors of the minesweeper HMS *Widnes* — the name of our hometown. She was sunk by bombs on one of our operations, but I did not know it at the time.

Gibraltar — always short and sweet and enjoyable. We saw a performance of *The Importance of Being Ernest*. The cast included Michael Wilding and Dame Edith Evans of 'Handbag' fame.

Bone — nothing really of interest, except for St Augustine's Cathedral, where there was a glass case containing the bones of a saint. To my amazement I met a former workmate who was in the Pioneer Corps, who was repairing the harbour wall. The army had staged a wonderful theatre show, but unfortunately we had to depart before the end as our leave had expired. The captain wrote to the army CO, apologising for our action and explaining that it was not the fault of the performers, who were great. I can still 'see' and 'hear' them now, reciting their version of 'There's a one-eyed yellow idol to the north of Khatmandu', and performing their pageant of 'Rose of England' when we had to leave. There were many occasions when we had to make our own entertainment, e.g. ship's concerts, which revealed some surprising talent. Then there was the cinema. At one time the entertainments officer wouldn't allow a war film to be shown. Instead they showed a western — *When the Daltons Rode*. There were more shootings and deaths in that film than in anything we had experienced. On another occasion, just after a film featuring Peter Cushing and some pickled brains, we went down to supper to find it consisted of sheep's brains.

The subject of the cinema reminds me that when in Brooklyn Navy Yard we were invited to see the movie shows aboard a new US battleship. We heard later that the crew refused to take her to sea until they had an ice-cream-making machine installed in place of an auxiliary boiler.

Algiers — we were there as AA defence. Nothing to get excited about — one sortie ashore was enough, though at last I had a meal with potato (I had forgotten the look and taste) along with roast beef, or was it camel? We were intrigued to see a column of legionnaires in all their glory, marching to their barracks.

There was one incident, which had nothing to do with the war and the enemy, but nevertheless caused great upset. It was here, so far as I remember, that the ship's cat fell into the harbour, between the ship and the jetty, causing panic among the crew. To the accompaniment of shouts of encouragement from ship and shore, some seamen climbed down; and, after some difficulty and resistance from the cat, she was safely rescued. Of course, in time-honoured naval tradition, she was duly reprimanded — "******!" — for leaving the ship without permission. As one would expect from a cat, she was completely nonchalant about the whole episode, devoured a saucer of milk and curled up and went to sleep. We could cope with bombs, shells, torpedoes, collisions, etc., but the cat falling into the harbour was quite a different matter — a really serious matter.

Malta — the island became very special to us as we had struggled so hard to save it — extra special to a few of us. I remember the plaque on the hillside along the road from the harbour to the city of Valletta, commemorating the bravery of a British regiment and HMS *Illustrious*, who fought so valiantly during the siege, when the local people very wisely hurried to the hillside caves for shelter. There are precious memories too of Floriana Methodist Church, where we had fellowship with dockyard workers, Wrens, members of other ships' crews and the army. Was it coincidence that the bells of the Roman Catholic church across the road would clang just as we started our evening service, or were they joining in our worship of thanksgiving? I kept in contact with some of the group long after the war.

I do not believe in coincidence — my belief is that such things are part of a plan for my life. Let me give you some examples:

(1) I had purchased some dress material I thought would come in useful to someone at home, but how or when was I to get it back to the UK? Another cruiser happened to be passing through on her way home, but I did not know until I saw him that an old schoolfriend (another ERA) was aboard. He promised to deliver it for me, and kept his promise. I have not seen him since, though I have seen his brother who comes into this story later.

(2) A short time later I met a group of sailors from *Black Swan*, and among them was my best pal from pre-war days, whom I hadn't seen for years, but had hoped would be best man at my wedding. Neither of us knew until that moment of each other's presence in Malta. A few minutes later we parted again to go our separate ways,

not knowing when or if we would meet again. With this in mind I had to choose another best man — Ray, a member of our fellowship group on *Dido*. Sadly, shortly after our return to UK and with my wedding day fast approaching, he was badly injured in a road accident and was in hospital for a long spell. What was I going to do now about a best man?

My fiancée and I went to see Ray's parents and, while waiting on a Manchester railway station, I saw a group of sailors who recognised me, though I did not recall knowing any of them until one called out, "Hi, Chief! Bill's home!"

'Bill who?' I thought. Then I realised it was the same group I had met from *Black Swan*, and Bill was my old mate, my original choice as best man.

The ship had just returned to the UK. Also, *Black Swan* was adopted by my hometown, Widnes, just as Bolton adopted *Dido*.

Furthermore, while I was home a young man overheard me talking about an incident at Anzio. "I remember that," he said. He was a junior engineer on a freighter we were shielding with a smokescreen during the landings. He was the brother of the ERA mentioned earlier. Coincidence? Not a bit of it!

Port Said — the least said about this place, the better — flea-ridden cinemas were one memory. Also, one of my messmates was robbed. The captain of another ship unwisely gave some of his crew members shore leave. The ship sailed the same day, but never reached her destination. Port Said was rife with supporters of the Axis, and it was dangerous to even whisper the slightest information about a ship's movements.

These are just a few of the places we visited. Others appear elsewhere in my narrative. We had seen a lot of the exotic Mediterranean, but everything was to change once again when we returned to the Home fleet and the familiar waters of Scapa Flow. There was leave, and, for four of the ERAs including myself, weddings. There was also the unwelcome change from the warm climate and relatively calm seas of the Mediterranean to the cold, windswept northern waters.

Whether in harbour or at sea, in the Arctic or Mediterranean regions, life on board never changes. When circumstances permitted, there were several businesses on board, which had to be officially approved. Amongst others were a photographer, who processed our shore-going snaps, and a snob (the naval term for a boot-repairer), who kept our footwear in good shape if he could.

Once he was asked, "Are you doing any snobbing today, Tom?"

"Naw, mite," he said, "I ain't got no niles, no levver, and no fread."

There was also a ship's barber, with a regular clientele. Some stokers set up a laundry business. We chiefs and POs appreciated that, but they had to be good or we wouldn't pay them.

Recreation included tombola (bingo). This was the only gambling game allowed, being organised by the entertainments committee, proceeds going into the ship's entertainment fund and to charity. (I think some was used to provide a Bolton children's party.) There were other games, such as uckers (ludo), with inter-mess tournaments. Cheating was rife, but, should anyone be caught, there was trouble. A very few played mah-jong (I don't know why) and there were dominoes. Card games were always popular and I became rather good at cribbage.

Handicrafts were useful, especially leatherwork; hobbies too — modelling in particular. The engineers' workshop was often busier between 4.00 p.m. and 8.00 p.m. than during working hours. This kept me occupied for a while. I was responsible for the lathes, etc., making sure they were used properly. There was always the library for less energetic souls — and there were many of those, some of them even disapproving of a number of the pastimes.

In harbour, fishing from the ship's side was popular; even Captain Terry joined in, when in the Med or the Red Sea. I hadn't the patience for it. Whenever we moved ship in Naples the order 'In all fishing lines' amused me. There were, of course, many of these lighter times in harbour. The ship's routine included the cleaning of the wooden decks by the seamen in the mornings. First they would scrub in one direction with their long-handled hard brooms, then back again. I was standing outside the motorboat workshop one morning and asked the chief PO in charge what they would do when they wore away the wood. His reply was to grab a broom and, to the delight of all present, chased me round the upper deck. I got back to the workshop just in time to prevent him using the broom on me — and he would have. I was reminded of this when, some years later, I was shown his photograph at a Bolton reunion.

Weekends were predictable. Saturday mornings saw captain's rounds. Everything had to be spotlessly clean, and the engine-room staff kept out of sight. All mess decks were inspected. What puzzled us was how some little-used equipment, hidden from the captain and his entourage, suddenly reappeared after rounds. Sunday mornings were invariably chaotic in the mess. There were so many of us in so little space. For divisions (i.e. captain's inspections), and perhaps a march past and church service on the quarterdeck, of course we had to wear our best suits.

Dressing was difficult at the best of times, but this was akin to bedlam, especially when one man exclaimed, "Oh bother! [*my* translation of the exact word used], I've dropped my collar stud." He then crawled around looking for it, causing no end of trouble. Miraculously, we managed to be ready in good time for the call at 09.50.

Occasionally, at 09.45 came the order, 'There will be no divisions,' no reason being given.

"Oh dear!" (my translation again) would be the reaction.

There were times when I was able to avoid this disorganised scrum, as I was in charge of the shore-going church parties, naturally leaving a little earlier. I knew some of the men only joined in to miss divisions, but that was their problem. I was twice, on returning to the ship, told to report to the engineer's office. The first time was to receive my MID certificate, which should have been officially presented to me at divisions. For that escape I was truly thankful. The second time I was asked why I had taken a church party ashore when I shouldn't have (leaving the ship without permission). The check of my service certificates revealed an error (?) in the religion column. I was advised to see the captain to have this corrected. This pleased everyone, except perhaps the chaplain.

On occasion, in Alexandria, when returning to the ship from across the harbour, we could see from the boat, the ship's company in a march past. The looks of relief on the faces of the church parties, mine included, were a joy to behold. I hated march pasts, though I did take part in a few on board, and they were a necessary part of discipline, in which I truly believe.

On one occasion, when entering harbour in Malta a marine fell overboard when fitting the accommodation ladder. He swam clear of the ship for his own safety, losing his cap in the process. Returning on board, he was charged with leaving the ship without permission and returning aboard improperly dressed (no cap!).

It would appear from much of this narrative that we were on a Cook's tour. Far from it. There was always the possibility of a recall or an emergency and a dash off to sea. For instance — after sudden preparation to escort another cruiser from Algiers to Gibraltar, we were not required. The other cruiser managed to reach Gibraltar and then the US with badly damaged bows — a great feat of seamanship. And, really, three days in Cairo, four in Asmara, two in Palestine and half a day in Pompeii, as well as harbour leave was not a lot in over three years. After all, we never knew which leave might be our last. So much for Admiral Cunningham's 'fleshpots of Alexandria', etc.

It was rather a shock to the system and detrimental to our well-being when we were recalled to the UK to rejoin the Home fleet. To go from the warm climate and relatively calm seas of the Med back to Atlantic gales and the North Sea and Arctic Ocean, was quite a contrast. Maybe the Admiralty, in their wisdom, thought that after our successes in the Med they would topple us from our pedestal; or perhaps shorten the war in Europe, which later proved to be the case.

The Russian convoys became of special interest to me. We managed a couple of hours ashore and saw the desolation of the wasteland and the abject poverty of the inhabitants. I met an airman/photographer from an accompanying escort carrier, and during our conversation it emerged that our fathers worked together back home — he already knew I was on *Dido*. We had quite a chat and amongst other things he told me the story of a pal who had been in hospital in North Russia. A Russian nurse was celebrating her birthday and the British servicemen/patients gave her some cigarettes. That was the last they saw of her as she had been transferred for fraternising with British sailors — so much for Anglo/Russian relations, as we discovered later.

The day before we left I received a request from another carrier to referee a football match between two Fleet Air Arm squadrons, to the annoyance of our torpedo officer, who was also a referee, and senior to me in that respect as well as rank. But for the intervention of my engineer officers, goodness knows what mischief he might have caused, as the rivalry between the gunnery and engineering departments still existed — another victory for the engine room. Maybe our commander (E) or the captain had words with him, as he left the ship shortly afterwards.

On our return to Scapa Flow, my photographer friend sent me some photos he had taken of *Dido* in the convoy. They were probably the only ones in existence.

Russian convoys did have their lighter moments as far as I was concerned. We sailed on October 21st 1944. "What better day than this, Trafalgar Day to set out for such an operation." So said our captain, John Terry. We did not share his sentiments.

Perhaps at this point I should explain briefly two of the traditions and customs of the Royal Navy:

(1) Every evening in harbour and at sea, the duty officer, in company with the duty petty officer, quartermaster, etc., toured the ship. Among their duties was the inspection of mess decks to check that all compartments not in use were locked and secure, with the respective keys in their racks; and then to report 'All present and correct.'

(2) The issue of cocoa to the night watches, i.e. midnight to 04.00 and 04.00 to 08.00. The seaman branch — gunners, telegraphers, etc. — had their cocoa (at least that's what they called it) issued from the galley, and by the time it reached the positions it was not very hot. We in the engine room were issued with a large, thick block of cocoa which the junior stoker would shred with a knife, adding a cup of sugar and a can of evaporated milk before transferring the mixture to a large can and boiling it with a steam jet. This was real cocoa.

However, when we sailed on this particular convoy our small group were holding our cabin fellowship when Bill told us the following story: Before the war he was serving in *Royal Oak* as chief electrical artificer. Late one afternoon the ship was loading torpedoes, when a young torpedoman decided to assist in the loading. Unfortunately, a torpedo swung round and knocked him down into the torpedo flat and he was killed. Naturally, work was stopped and all compartments locked and secured.

At midnight a telegrapher sitting at the switchboard noticed the torpedo-flat light flickering. When he took the call a voice said, "I am the ghost of the torpedo flat. Where's my cocoa? I haven't had my cocoa."

Somewhat startled, he reported the incident to the officer of the watch, who immediately investigated, taking the torpedo-flat keys with him. All was secure and there was no sign of human presence around. So where did the voice come from? Shortly afterwards, Bill and a workmate were working late in their workshop near the torpedo flat when they heard a thud on the deck, looked around, and seeing nothing decided it must be the ship's cat. When they realised the ship didn't have a cat they didn't stay a moment longer and never worked late there again. Bill was promoted to the rank of warrant officer and left the ship. We shall never know what really happened as *Royal Oak* was sunk early in the war. So the ghost was laid to rest — or was it?

Within a few hours of hearing this story I was on watch in the after engine room when at about 0.45 hours a telephone rang, and as I picked up the handset I heard a slow, melancholy, drawling voice say, "Chief, where's my cocoa? I haven't had my cocoa yet. I want my cocoa."

Not quite settled down, I froze for a few seconds and a stoker remarked, "What's the matter, Chief? You look as though you've just seen a ghost."

"No," I said, "I've just spoken to one." I went over to the junior stoker responsible for this joke, and though I cannot recall what I said to him, he was very quickly on his way there and back again.

Weatherwise, the return trip was much livelier; the ship was bouncing, twisting, turning, heaving, rolling, pitching — everything but flying. On a Sunday afternoon, almost at the end of my watch, there was a loud crash and bang on the ship's side and water cascaded in through the air intakes. The engine-room deck was awash and one or two men were soaked — a most uncomfortable few minutes. We learned later that a heavy sea had washed right over us. There are better ways to end a watch.

On another watch I noticed a stoker gazing at me intently, as he shaved a stick with his penknife. "Eh," he said, "I could make thee a lovely coffin." I learned later that he came from an undertaker's family. If he's still waiting for me he'll have to wait for a while yet.

With Norwegian air strikes we encountered the worst seas ever, in both the Atlantic and Arctic Oceans. Our station, most times, was astern of the aircraft carrier. At one time the full length of her flight deck could be seen, then the propellers were almost clear of the water. Many ships were damaged by the weather and others were recalled to Scapa — but not gallant little *Dido*, even though we were tossed all over the place and admonished by the carrier for not keeping station. Meals were non-existent for days at a time, as some galleys could not be used. It would have been a waste of food anyway, for many, including the captain, were seasick. This was one time when I thought the words from the Naval Prayer, " ... from the dangers of the sea, and from the violence of the enemy ... "

should read, "... from the violence of the sea, and from the dangers of the enemy ..."

On our return to harbour, we were visited by the padre of a similar cruiser who remarked, "It was all right for us, we were called back in, but you in poor old *Dido* had to stay out in it."

We were out of favour with the Admiralty again. Perhaps they thought we had been on a picnic in the Med. Their sense of humour was not appreciated. We did have our just rewards — first Copenhagen and the end of the war in Europe. Then we played host to Their Majesties twice, taking them to the Isle of Man and on their visit to Rosyth.

No matter how efficient and well drilled a ship may be, there will be occasions when chaos is the order of the day. 'Ammunition ship' (in which stokers joined at times) caused much shouting and clatter. 'Oiling ship' was another matter. The only time the seamen 'helped' the stokers was to complain if one drop of oil was spilled on their precious deck. One day the chief stoker in charge wrote down the total quantity of oil in each tank, then totalled the list. For a while he panicked, as the total showed more than the ship could carry; then he realised that he had added in the date which he had written at the top of his sheet of paper. Oiling from shorelines or a tanker alongside took but a few hours — at Kola Bay it took more than twenty. There were no pumps, so oil was literally poured in from barrels. By this time *Apollo* and Co. had finished their minelaying and were awaiting our reappearance. 'Paint Ship' was another chore. Over the years, I think we must have used enough paint to reinforce the armour plating.

There was one job, which I hated, that seemed to be allocated regularly. When in dry dock, the ship's seacocks had to be connected to water supplies. This meant working on the dry dock and fitting 'flooding bonnets' over the sea inlets and hoses attached to the shore supplies. "What! Me again?" would be my reaction, but to no avail. At least I was not crawling about in a boiler, although, unlike some, I was just built for that, and I did have my share of it in my early days in the ship. However, it did add variety to what was an eventful experience.

Many times I have chuckled over incidents in the ship, but there is one that saddens and haunts me — Crete — though that was more than compensated for by the 'Happy and Glorious' end at Copenhagen.

Luckily, I was never seasick, but when I left the Royal Navy —

again at the behest of HM Government — I was sick of the sea, or was I? As a member of the Royal Naval Reserve, I was recalled to the service for a year and a half during the Korean War period. During this time, while serving in HMS *Obedient,* I last saw *Dido.* We attended the Coronation Review in 1953. She was then the flagship of the reserve fleet, whose commanding officer was Admiral (by that time) McCall. This second spell in the navy caused me, to quote my wife, "to have itchy feet," as I later applied to join the Royal New Zealand Navy and was accepted for six years' service. But that is another story, except to mention that I was to meet up again with several ex-*Dido* engine-room colleagues, even one on a visiting RN destroyer, who had, though unknown to me at the time, served a second term on *Dido* at the review. He was the last ex-*Dido* colleague I was to meet until the 1991 Bolton reunion.

An important, probably the most important, thing to a serviceman serving abroad is the regular delivery of mail from home. This is especially true of the navy — because we moved around so much we never knew how, when or where, or even if, we would receive the next delivery. When it was received it always produced a mixture of highs and lows, of which I had my own share. In September 1941, on arrival in New York, I was greeted by the news that my brother had become the father of a daughter. Almost exactly a year later, when the ship arrived back in Alexandria from Haifa, there was, on top of my mail pile, a letter from the same brother telling me that on the advice of his doctor he was to go into hospital for an operation. The last piece of news was a telegram to say he had died. I was completely shattered, and for the next few days I slept and ate very little, though fortunately it did not affect my work or duties. Then I realised how other men must have felt when they heard of family members killed in air raids — so far away and nothing one could do to alleviate the grief. So cruel!

There were many letters causing distress because of long separation from families. I spoke to one messman: "You're not looking too happy, Geordie."

"My wife's just had a babby." *(sic)*

"Shouldn't you be happy?"

"Would you be if it was a little black ******. "

He had been away a long time and a so-called friend had written to him, which was the first he had heard about it. I talked to him for a while and he decided to see the captain to request compassionate leave, which was granted.

One of my messmates was a keen Bing Crosby fan, and would turn up the volume on the radio whenever a Crosby record was played. We tolerated this because he always reduced the sound again, but one evening a Crosby record was greeted with silence. Why? We discovered he had received a dreaded Dear John letter. Distance and time had discouraged his fiancée. These are some examples of the heartache that can be the result of navy life — happily not too often, and for some of us it was rather 'Absence makes the heart grow fonder', as it was for me.

During my service in *Dido* I can recall more than sixty chiefs and ERAs joining and leaving. They came from all parts of the UK and even from Canada. With perhaps thirty men crammed into the confined space of a small mess, and given such diverse backgrounds and lifestyles, it was inevitable there would be wide differences of opinion — North versus South, Scots versus everyone else, etc. Naturally there were arguments, but happily they never lasted long, and in fact I cannot recall any real acrimony. By and large they were a great group of men, given the trying and frustrating conditions we had to endure. I was proud to be one of them.

My last recollection was of Weymouth beach. As the ship was based in Portland, Weymouth was one of the 'watering places' for the ship's company. Out of the sixty names I can remember, only two come to mind out of our party of twelve that night. I wonder why? But they were true comrades and I respect them for that.

These are but a selection of my memories of my time on *Dido*. There are far too many for me to record here. Bill once said to me, "You know, most of all, this will be just fragrant memories." How very true! Like all ex-servicemen my memories are endless, but I have tried to avoid being boring by including only the most interesting ones. Many of the memories are fragrant, especially of Malta, the Holy Land and most of all Copenhagen.

A final memory is of Scapa Flow. In foul weather, ships at anchor were required to raise steam and prepare for sea in case of an emergency, such as dragging anchor. During the midnight watch the watchkeepers were relaxing, when quite unexpectedly the duty engineer officer entered the engine room from the after end, instead of the usual forward end, and saw one or two men sitting down (not allowed). He had obviously spent too much time in the wardroom. However, he asked, "Don't you chaps have anything to eat?"

"No, sir," was the reply, at which he disappeared, to return moments later with a loaf of bread. An ERA and a stoker were despatched to their respective quarters for a tin of jam and some butter. That was the only midnight feast I have heard of taking place in an engine room. The incident certainly didn't reach the ears of the senior engineer, in which case there would have been real trouble, as a few of us, including myself, had incurred his displeasure in an earlier incident. This was to be one of my last watchkeeping duties on the ship, as we sailed shortly afterwards for Portland and my farewell to the Royal Navy.

Finally, may I say, Bolton, you have every reason to be proud of your ship, my ship, OUR SHIP.

HMS *DIDO*
War Service

July 1939	Launched at Birkenhead.
Sept 1940	Commissioned at Birkenhead.
Sept 1940	"Working Up" *Scapa Flow*. High-speed sweeps off Fair Isle and Greenland.
Nov 1940	Escorted *Furious* to West Africa, ferrying aircraft which were later used in Wavell's Africa attack.
Jan - Apr 1941	Atlantic convoys.
April 1941	Ran stores to *Malta* — joined Eastern Mediterranean fleet.
May 1941	Destroyed enemy invasion force against *Crete* and covered evacuation of the island.
May 29th 1941	Badly damaged by bombs while taking troops from *Crete* to *Alexandria*.
June 8th 1941	*Dido*'s marines accepted surrender of *Assab*.
July - Nov 1941	Refitted in Brooklyn Navy Yard.
Dec 1941	Rejoined Eastern Mediterranean forces.
Jan - Mar 1942	Covered convoys between *Alexandria* and *Malta*.
Mar 14th 1942	Bombarded *Rhodes*.
Mar 22nd 1942	*Battle of Sirte*.
Apr - Sept 1942	Supported army against Rommel's advance on *Egypt*.
Oct Nov 1942	Supported advance of 8th Army from *El Alamein*. Last bombardment of *Tobruk* to allow army to enter.

Dec 1942	Joined Western Mediterranean squadron.
Dec 1942 - Mar 1943	AA guard at *Bone* and *Algiers*
Apr - June 1943	Refitted at Liverpool.
June 27th 1943	Rejoined Western Mediterranean squadron.
July 1943	Took part in diversionary bombardments against *N. Sicily* and the *Catalanian* coast during landings in *Sicily*.
Aug - Sept 1943	Based at *Palermo* and *Bizerta* as AA guards for invasion bases.
Sept 12th 1943	Sailed with 600 airborne troops to occupy *Taranto*. Italian fleet surrendered.
Sept 16th - 28th 1943	Bombarded in support of the army at *Salerno*.
Oct - Nov 1943	Refitted at Alexandria.
Dec 1943 - Jan 1944	At *Malta* and *Taranto*.
Jan 22nd 1944	Created diversion of *Civitavecchia*, during initial landing at *Anzio*.
Jan - May 1944	Bombarded in support of the army at *Anzio* and *Formia*.
June - July 1944	At *Naples* and *Alexandria*.
July 24th 1944	Fleet reviewed by His Majesty the King in *Naples Bay*.
Aug 1944	Supported landings in *Southern France* from base in *Corsica*.
Sept 1944	Returned to the United Kingdom.
Oct 1944	Escorted Russian convoy.
Nov 1944 - Apr 1945	Supported carrier strikes off *Norway*.
Apr 1945	Escorted *Apollo*, *Orwell* and *Obedient* minelaying in *North Kola Inlet*.
May 1945	Arrived at *Copenhagen* (firing — en route — the last shot in the war in Europe). Escorted surrendered German cruisers, *Prinz Eugen* and *Nurnberg,* to *Wilhelmshaven*. The surrender was signed aboard *Dido*.
July 1945	Conveyed Their Majesties to the Isle of Man.

Total Miles Steamed	145,000
Total 5.25 Rounds Fired in Action	30,000+